A BOOK TO BEGIN ON

LIGHTS

by Margaret C. Farquhar

Illustrated by Tom Funk

Holt, Rinehart and Winston   New York

FLICK!
The lights are out.
The electricity is off.
QUICK!
Where is the flashlight?
Light a match.
Light a candle.
Light a kerosene lamp.
Now you can see!

What if we had no electric lights?
What if we had no candles?
What if we had no matches?
What if we had no kerosene?
What if we had no lights at all?

Long, long ago the sun gave the
only light by day.

The moon and stars gave the only
light by night.

There were no plants,
No animals,
No men on the earth.

Plants and animals began to grow
first in the seas.

Later some of the animals crawled
onto the land.

Plants and trees began to grow on
the land, too.

Sometimes clouds covered the sun.

Sometimes they covered the moon and stars.

Then the days were dark.

The nights were black.

CRACK!
Sometimes lightning flashed light across the sky.

Once in a while the lightning set
fire to the trees.
There was no one on the earth to
put out the fires.

Millions and millions of years
later the first men appeared.
They lived in caves like animals.

The cave men could hide in their caves.

They could hide from animals and forest fires.

They were afraid of fire.

But fire could help them.

Fire kept them warm.

It cooked the animal meat.

It lighted their caves.

The cave men kept a fire burning day and night.

What happened when the fire went out?

They had to find a way of making fire.

They may have rubbed a stick hard against a soft piece of wood.

RUB! RUB! RUB!

Heat from the rubbing made a spark!

The wood dust caught fire.

Fan the fire! Feed it with dry leaves and twigs!

The cave men made torches by
setting fire to long sticks.

The torches lighted their way at
night.

Now they could hunt wild animals at night.

Later cave men made lamps.
They made light holders of
  animal skulls,
    sea shells,
      hollow stones.

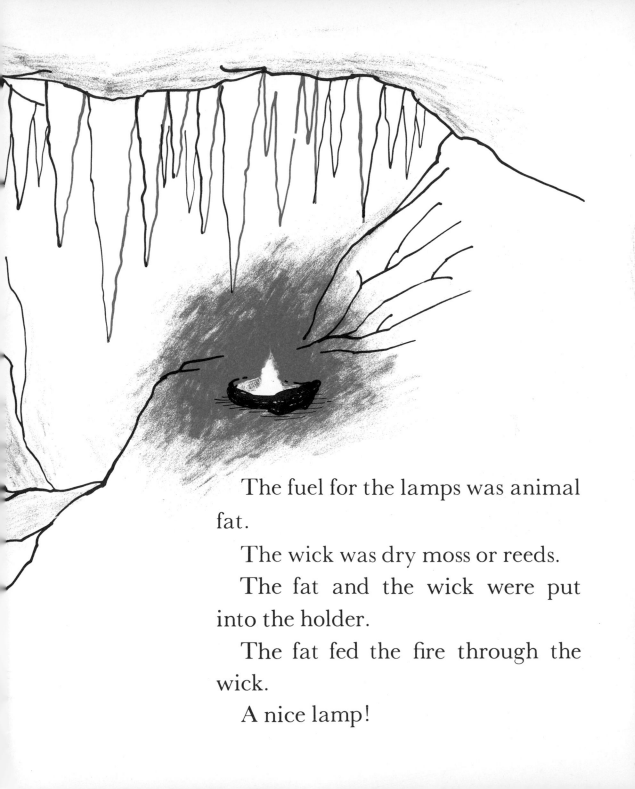

The fuel for the lamps was animal fat.

The wick was dry moss or reeds.

The fat and the wick were put into the holder.

The fat fed the fire through the wick.

A nice lamp!

Men began to draw pictures on the walls of their caves.

Later men drew pictures and signs on blocks of stones and on dried animal skins.

The pictures and signs told stories.

They were the beginnings of reading and writing.

Years and years went by.

Men read and wrote more.

They needed better lights.

The Egyptians made lamps of copper and gold. They made the wicks of woven cotton.

The cotton wick in melted fat burned longer than the moss and reed wicks.

Men were writing more and more.

They needed better light.

The Greeks and Romans made student lamps.

They made lamps of clay and metal. They put decorations on them.

They used olive oil for fuel.

They put spouts on the lamps to keep the flame burning evenly.

The Egyptians knew the secret of making candles and torches.

They made their candles by dipping long reeds into animal fat.

They made torches by soaking balls of rags in oil and fastening these with wire to the ends of metal rods.

Slaves carried the torches to light processions.

In the Middle Ages men learned ways of making better candles.

There were traveling candle-makers.

They used cotton and linen string for the wicks.

Some made tallow candles by dipping the strings in melted animal fat.

Some made wax candles of melted beeswax.

Not many people could buy the wax candles in those days. They cost two pennies apiece!

Candles and torches were put on candle sticks and in holders.

They lighted houses, castles, and churches for hundreds of years.

Out-of-doors men carried candles in metal boxes with thin pieces of cow horn on the sides.

Wind could not blow out the flame.

The pieces of cow horn were like windows for the light to shine through.

Men used to call the candle boxes lamp horns. We call them lanterns now.

Lamp horns were hung on door-ways to light the streets.

When the Pilgrims came to America they brought Betty lamps with them.

The first Betty lamps were made of iron.

They looked like the old Roman lamps with noses or spouts for the cloth wicks to rest in.

The Pilgrims burned fish and whale oil in their lamps.

The light was so poor they could hardly see to spin or read the Bible.

Firelight from pine logs made a better light.

The log cabins were smoky and not much lighter than the cave man's home.

Candles gave a better light than Betty lamps.

The Pilgrims made their own candles.

They dipped long strands of yarn into kettles of melted fat.

DIP. COOL.

DIP. COOL.

DIP. COOL.

Dipping the candle made it the right size.

Some of the Pilgrims had candle molds.

They poured tallow and beeswax into the candle molds.

They poured candles of melted bayberries, too.

What a sweet smell!

The Pilgrims and their children were good candlemakers.

Later men discovered that oil
lamps with two wicks gave a stead-
ier and brighter light than those
with just one.

But still they had no matches to
light their lamps. They only had
tinderboxes.

The tinderbox contained cloth for
tinder, steel, and flint.

Men rubbed the steel and flint
together,
    blew the spark,
        set fire to the tinder.

Millions of years ago the cave
men had made fire in much the
same way.

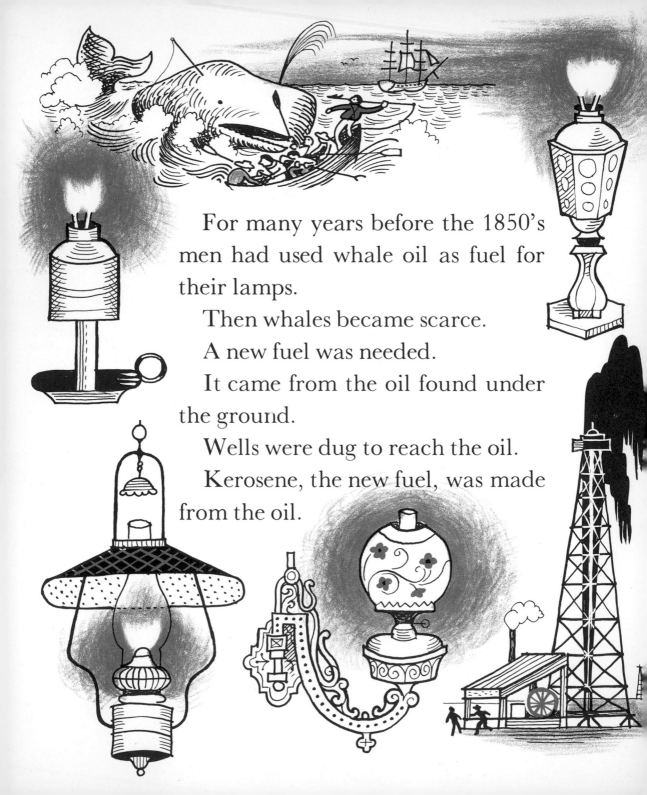

For many years before the 1850's men had used whale oil as fuel for their lamps.

Then whales became scarce.

A new fuel was needed.

It came from the oil found under the ground.

Wells were dug to reach the oil.

Kerosene, the new fuel, was made from the oil.

Kerosene lamps were the first ones to have chimneys made of glass.

The glass chimney protected the flame.

It let all the light shine through, unlike the lamp horns.

The cotton wick in the kerosene lamp could be turned up to make a brighter light.

Safety matches were invented! Kerosene lamps were easy to light.

Another kind of fuel for lamps was found under the ground.

It came from coal, made by plants and trees buried underground for millions of years.

A gas fuel was made when the coal was heated.

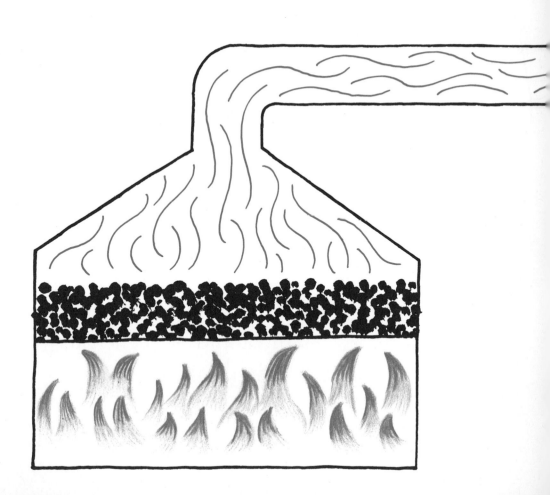

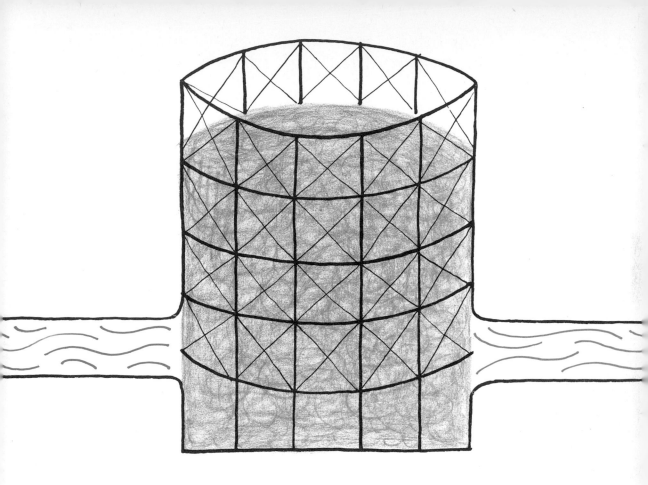

You cannot see coal gas.

You can smell it.

You can burn it.

It makes a yellow light.

Big furnaces heated coal to make
the gas.

Then it was stored in tanks.

The gas was sent through pipes to cities and houses.

Gas was burned for many years in street and house lamps.

It gave a steady, brighter light than kerosene.

Children could see better to do their school work.

U. S. 1181830

Ever since the days of cave men
the fuel for lights had to be burned.
The flames were dangerous.
They used air to burn.
Rooms became airless.
There needed to be a better way
of lighting.

For many years men had tried to make use of electricity.

They had learned to make electric batteries with chemicals and metals.

Then came the electric arc lamp!

A giant spark jumped between two carbon rods when electricity ran through them.

The carbon arc lights made fine street lamps but they were too bright for houses. They flickered too.

Thomas Edison had experimented for many years to find a better way of lighting houses.

His first lamp in 1879 looked like a hairpin loop in a bottle.

The loop was heated by an electric current.

The loop became white from the heat. It gave off light!

Edison had machinery built to keep electricity running through the wire loop in his bulb.

He invented light sockets,
light switches,
fuses.

Wires leading from a powerhouse carried electricity to light the bulbs.

New York in 1882 was the first city to have a powerhouse.

People saw electric light gave a clear, soft, steady light.

It was safe. A flick of a switch lit a lamp. No matches were needed. No lamp fuel burned in the air.

Electric light did not cost much.

Soon powerhouses were built to light cities, towns, and villages all over the country.

Electricity is still our best lighting fuel. In some of our newer electric lights we use gas. Neon gas found in the air is one kind we use.

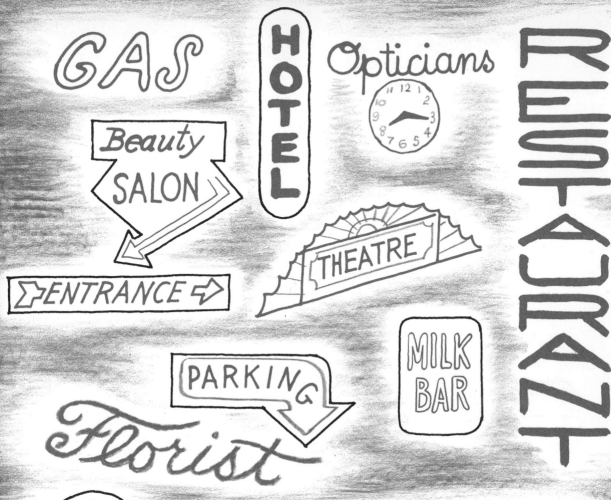

A neon lamp gives a bright red light when electricity is turned on.

Because it is so bright neon can be seen from far off. It is used for outdoor advertising in store windows and signs.

It is also used in piloting planes.

There are chemicals as well as gases in the fluorescent lamp.

They glow when electricity runs through them.

There are no wires in the lamp to give off heat.

The light is a cool one.

A fluorescent lamp can light a large room better than many small bulbs.

It makes a good light for kitchens.
We use it to light office buildings and factories.

Some day houses may have lights like these.

Glass panels are on the walls.

The glass is coated with chemicals.

It is electricity that makes the chemicals glow.

CLICK.
The light is white.
You can read.
CLICK. CLICK.
The light is rosy.
Cozy in winter!
CLICK. CLICK. CLICK.
The light is blue.
So cool in summer!

The cave man would be surprised to see the many kinds of lights we can use today.

But we may be surprised to see the kind of lights our children and grandchildren will be using.

Men are good inventors!